SHELLS

SHELLS

CLARE NICHOLSON

PHOTOGRAPHS BY DEBBIE PATTERSON

LORENZ BOOKS

NEW YORK • LONDON • SYDNEY • BATH

This edition published in 1996 by Lorenz Books
an imprint of Anness Publishing Limited
administrative office: 27 West 20th Street
New York, NY 10011

Lorenz Books are available for bulk purchase for sales promotion and for premium use.
For details write or call the manager of special sales, LORENZ BOOKS, 27 West 20th Street,
New York, NY 10011; (212) 807-6739.

Produced by Anness Publishing Limited
1 Boundary Row
London SE1 8HP

ISBN 1 85967 149 7 X

Publisher: Joanna Lorenz
Senior editor: Clare Nicholson
Special photography: Debbie Patterson
Step photography: Lucy Tizard
Designer: Lilian Lindblom
Illustrations: Lucinda Ganderton

Printed in Singapore by
Star Standard Industries Pte Ltd

CONTENTS

INTRODUCTION

T he delicate creamy pink tones and fantastically varied shapes of shells have fascinated the seashore-dwelling people of the world ever since they thought to embellish anything. They have made jewelry with them, used them for embroidery, decorated homes and furniture with them, and even used them in their natural state as containers. Part of the fascination has to be that these delicately colored, delicate-looking forms are, in fact, incredibly resilient. Designed as the homes of creatures which have to withstand very rough conditions indeed, many of them are more than up to coping with the wear and tear of a land-dweller's life. Compared with surging seas and the risks of being smashed against jagged rocks, decoratively gracing a garden over winter in northern Europe is hardly a problem. This has made shells a wonderful medium for decorating almost everything from an outdoor gazebo to an ornamental box. The Victorians loved to decorate, and shells were a favorite material. They encrusted boxes, mirrors and picture frames with them and they made pictures and grottoes with them. On the other side of the world, tiny polished shells decorated clothes; larger ones were prized for currency.

As well as the shells themselves, the advent of holidays spawned a love of all things seashore. The paraphernalia of flotsam and jetsam and the images of sea creatures, rope, netting, and boats, evoked the ambience of the sunny days on the beach when summer has passed. The shell image has never lost its appeal. Their sheer variety is extraordinary, ranging from smooth whelks, cones, and cowries with their naturally polished shells to elongated spindles and tibia, curled-up conches and spiky, comblike murex shells. Then there are the flattened shells, such as cockles, clams and abalones with their iridescent insides. No wonder they've captured our imagination.

If you want to use the real thing, beachcombing is one of the most enjoyable and

ecological ways of collecting shells, since the inhabitants of those washed up on the shore have usually already left home. The best time to collect is after a storm when the waves have brought the bounty in, and before others have plundered it. However, be careful of beachcombing when you're on vacation. Some countries do not allow anything to be taken off their beaches, so check first. There are several outlets which sell shells from all over the world, and many of them have been collected so as not to affect the ecological balance.

Check with the supplier before you buy. Many bags of shells are labeled to indicate they have been responsibly collected. Another ecologically sound way of shell collecting is to buy shell-

Above: Wood panel from Chancay, Peru, with shell decoration on the eyes and neckpiece.
Center: Goldwork caracole from Colombia.

fish to eat. Mussels, scallops, clams, and oysters all have wonderful shells that can be used effectively. Fishmongers sometimes have scallop shells to spare, but you may have to buy the others for dinner, then use the shells afterwards. They're not expensive when they are in season.

Shells come in a really wonderful variety of shapes and sizes, so they also make terrific motifs for decorating other materials. Scallop shells, for example, with their simple shape that is easy to define, have been the most widely reproduced as a motif. They were used as the badge of a pilgrim during the Middle Ages, and sometimes appeared in religious art, such as in the *Donor Before Virgin* from the *Forster Book of Hours* (see page 11). They are commonly seen as the inspiration for a series of curves along the edges of fabrics and they are featured in nursery rhymes. Starfish, whelks, conelike top shells, and spindle-like augers, also have simple graphic shapes that make successful decoration.

Above: Shells from Albert Seba's Locupletissimi Rerum Naturalium, *c.1750.*

But the most beautiful shell, and the one that has captured the imagination of artists through the centuries, must be the nautilus with its creamy, curled form that sometimes comes with a pearly sheen. Trace out simple outlines, following the form of the real shell or copy the outline from an illustration to make templates that can be used for appliqué and embroidery. Make potato or lino cuts for stamping and stencils for decorative paint effects.

If exotic shells are hard to find, and you'd like more detail than simple outlines, search out black-and-white line illustrations from old reference books or exquisitely hand-colored prints then, either use the originals or photocopy them to use for collage and découpage.

Center: Art nouveau three-legged stand with shell motif from Chihuahua, Mexico. Designed by La Torre 1907-10.

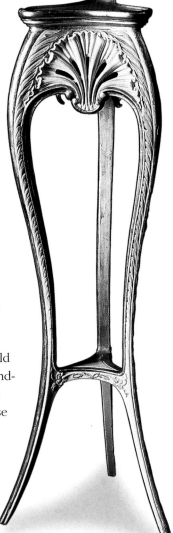

The photocopier is a wonderful modern tool for arts and crafts of all kinds because you can enlarge and reduce or even stretch the images, then use combinations to make up new designs.

The natural colors of shells in creamy white, pink, apricot, beige and tan always look wonderful together. They work very well set against the natural colors of rocks and sand, ranging from white to charcoal gray.

For sculptures, search out flotsam and jetsam from the beach, such as driftwood, pebbles and fishing net and rope. For needlecrafts, you could look for natural undyed fabric such as muslin, calico, canvas and burlap. As an alternative you may like to set the shells against the seawater shades of blue and green. These look particularly effective when used in layers, one on top of the other.

Left: The scallop shell was worn as the badge of a pilgrim, as seen here in the Forster Book of Hours. *Below: Detail of fountain of terracotta, ceramic plates, shells and tiles in San Angel, Mexico.*

For needlework items, try using translucent iridescent fabrics such as metal shot organdies, then embroidering or appliquéing shells on top. For decorative paintwork, use translucent glazes tinted with shades of azure, turquoise and lapis lazuli. This book is packed with inspiration, showing you how to make exquisite gifts, using shells and their images in a wide variety of materials and using various skills and techniques. You may like to learn new skills, or work in a medium which you are confident in following the instructions exactly, or substituting the materials or adapting the design, if you like, to suit your own style. However you like to work, the result will be beautiful one-off treasures to keep and display or to give to friends as presents.

PINPRICKED LAMPSHADE

This technique is most effective on a neutrally colored paper shade with a smooth surface, so avoid dark colors. When the lamp is lit, the pattern glows and makes a real focal point for the room. Do not use this technique on a fabric or a fabric-covered shade.

YOU WILL NEED

MATERIALS
lampshade

EQUIPMENT
soft and hard pencils
tracing paper
white paper
scissors
masking tape
towel
heavy-duty darning needle
thimble
heavy construction paper
  (optional)

1 Trace the template from the back of the book, and enlarge it, if necessary. Copy it several times. Cut the motifs roughly out.

2 Use masking tape to place the motifs in a pleasing pattern all around the shade to give you positioning guides.

3 Transfer the motif onto tracing paper, and rub over the reverse with a soft pencil. Trace the motif on the inside of the shade, following the positioning guides. Draw on any extra patterning. Remove the copies from the outside.

4 Resting the shade on a towel, prick out the motif from the wrong side, so that tiny bumps appear on the surface. You may practice on heavy construction paper first, to get the right feel and to check that the motif is suitable.

EMBROIDERED UNDERWATER PICTURE

The effect of the layers of blue and green organdy is marvelously evocative of an undersea scene. This tranquil picture would be ideal for hanging in a bedroom, where its calm, reflective quality is bound to induce sweet dreams.

YOU WILL NEED

MATERIALS
shades of green and blue shot organdy
metallic organdy
shot velvets
shot silk
shot organdy
pearlized lamé
metallic embroidery threads

EQUIPMENT
scissors
straight pins
embroidery hoop
white paper
sewing machine with embroidery foot

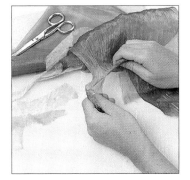

1 Use one sheet of organdy as the base of the sea. Tear strips of organdy to form the sea background.

2 Assemble all the strips, and pin them together. Fit them neatly into the hoop. Pin them in place.

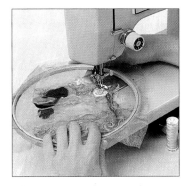

3 Make shell-, fish- and starfish-paper templates. Cut out shells from the metallic organdy, fish from the velvets and silk, and starfish from the shot organdy and lamé. Pin and machine stitch to the background, using metallic threads.

4 Build up the design with texture and color. Remove the embroidery from the hoop, and stretch it back into shape. Now it's ready for framing.

SHELL DISPLAY CASE

A purpose-made unit that suits the scale of shells and echoes their sinewy curves in its shape, is the perfect way of displaying beautiful shells. The glowing aquamarine color sets off the tints of the shells and is a reminder of the water that is their natural setting. The gold decoration, like sunlight on water, is the perfect finishing touch.

YOU WILL NEED

MATERIALS
modeling clay
acrylic paints: turquoise, white
  and lemon yellow
gold powder
clear matte varnish
selection of seashells
epoxy resin glue

EQUIPMENT
thin cardboard or paper
rolling pin
polyethylene sheet (optional)
modeling tools
paint-mixing container
small flat-bristled and fine
  paintbrushes

1 Trace the template from the back of the book, and enlarge it, if necessary. Roll out the clay in the shape of the swirl, to a thickness of about ⅓ in. You may find it helpful to work on a sheet of polyethylene.

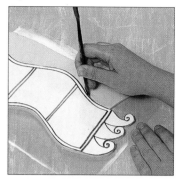

2 Lay the template on the clay and, with a wet modeling tool, cut out the shape for the back of the unit.

3 Roll out long, clay snakes, and cut them into rectangles about 1 in wide, with perfectly straight edges to make the side walls. Attach the walls to the back, molding and smoothing the joint with a wet modeling tool. Make a hole for hanging in the middle "wave" at the top.

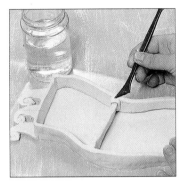  

4 Roll out and cut shorter rectangles for the shelves, and attach them to the back and the walls. Use a small piece of clay, smoothed over the joints to strengthen them. Allow to dry out for 2–3 days.

5 Mix the acrylic paints to make a sea-green color. To achieve a slight verdigris effect do not mix the colors too thoroughly. Paint the inside and outside of the display unit, and allow to dry.

6 Mix the gold powder with varnish, varying the amount of varnish depending on the consistency you wish to achieve. Paint the edges of the display case and the waves gold, using a fine paintbrush.

7 Working from the top down, arrange the shells in the compartments, and glue them in position.

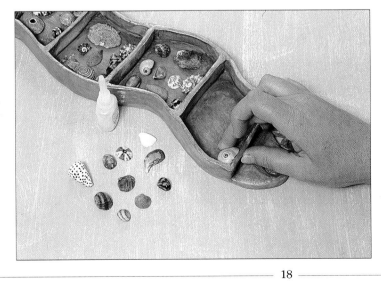

SILK-PAINTED SHEER CURTAIN

This sheer curtain is an unusual alternative to nets, allowing in the light, yet masking the window. Gutta forms a strong outline that stops the silk paints from bleeding into one another. It also creates a graphic outline, similar to stained-glass windows.

YOU WILL NEED

MATERIALS
white cotton cheesecloth fabric, to fit the window
gutta
iron-fixed silk paints: deep blue, bright green and yellow
strong sewing thread
½ in cotton hemming tape
curtain-weighting cord

EQUIPMENT
thin cardboard or paper
lining paper
clear plastic sheeting
masking tape
pipette with a fine nib
paint-mixing containers
fine paintbrushes
iron and pressing cloth
spray starch
sewing machine
needle

1 Trace the templates from the back of the book, and enlarge them, if necessary. Cut the lining paper, plastic sheeting, and the fabric to fit your window. Arrange the templates on the paper, and draw around them. Then draw seaweed, freehand, to pull the design together. Put the plastic on top and the fabric on top of that. Secure with masking tape.

2 Apply the gutta to the cheesecloth fabric, using the pipette, following the outlines on the lining paper. Press firmly. It is important for the gutta line to be solid to prevent the paint from bleeding. Check for any gaps or thin lines.

3 When the gutta is dry, paint in the colored areas with the silk paints. Allow to dry.

▶

4 Iron the curtain, to fix the paints, according to the manufacturer's instructions. Wash the curtain and apply spray starch when it's dry.

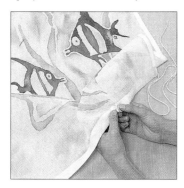

5 Apply the hemming tape to finish and neaten the edges. Insert the weighting cord in the bottom hem. Make a casing for the heading by turning over the edge and applying hemming tape to the seam.

HAND-PRINTED SEAWEED GIFT WRAP

Swirling seaweed shapes in watery shades of green and blue, on a blue-green background, produce an underwater effect that makes a really unusual gift wrapping paper. Vary the colors of the paints depending on the color of the background paper you choose.

YOU WILL NEED

MATERIALS
blue-green wrapping paper
acrylic paints: sap green, white and blue

EQUIPMENT
thin cardboard or paper
fine black felt-tipped pen
acetate sheet
craft knife
self-healing cutting mat
paint-mixing container
stencil brushes

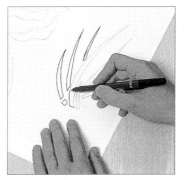

1 Trace the templates A, B and C from the back of the book, and enlarge them, if necessary. Go over the outline with the black pen. Lay the acetate on top and carefully cut the stencil, using a cutting mat to protect the work surface.

2 Position the stencil on the wrapping paper. Mix sap-green paint with a little white. Using a stencil brush, stencil templates A and B side by side in rows across the paper, leaving space for a row of template C between them.

3 With white, add highlights to the seaweed tips.

4 Mix blue paint with white, and stencil C in rows, leaving a stencil space in between for light-blue seaweeds.

SEA-TONED PILLOWCASE

Rainbow yarn, in which a variety of beautifully toning shades is combined in one length, is couched with matching embroidery thread to create lovely sea-toned shell shapes on this pillowcase.

YOU WILL NEED

MATERIALS
pillowcase, with flanges and decorative embroidery line
iron-on interfacing
rainbow yarn
pale-blue and blue-green embroidery threads
dark-blue stranded embroidery threads

EQUIPMENT
tracing paper or thin paper
straight pins
transfer pen
small, fine embroidery needle
tapestry or large-eyed needle
iron

1 Trace the shell motif from the back of the book, and enlarge it, if necessary. Mark the positions of the shell motifs on the pillowcase with pins. Transfer to the pillowcase.

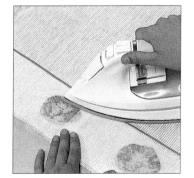

3 Using a large-eyed needle, pull the ends through to the wrong side. Iron interfacing on to secure.

2 Cut the rainbow yarn into separate colors. Use a single strand of pale blue to couch the blue threads, and the same of blue-green for the green-blue shades. Couch a single pale-blue thread between the bands of color.

4 Weave a thread of dark blue through the decorative stitching to finish it off.

SEASHELL CANDLE POT

There is nothing like candlelight and, for a room with a maritime theme, this candle pot is the perfect finishing touch. It would make an ideal center-piece for a table because it looks good all the way around and isn't too high. A variety of seashells and dried flowers can be used. Just make sure that you get a balance of materials in color, form, and texture. Remember never to leave burning candles unattended.

You WILL NEED

MATERIALS
thick candle
florist's tape
mossing pins or stub wires
oasis
flowerpot
moss
seashells
starfish
dried flowerheads

EQUIPMENT
knife
glue gun

1 Stick tape all around the base of the candle. Then hold three evenly spaced mossing pins or bent stub wires against the tape, and tape over them to hold them in position.

2 Trim the oasis to fit tightly in the pot. Push it in, and secure it firmly with some of the leftover pieces. Push the pins into the oasis to hold the candle firmly.

3 Glue the moss around the candle. Then add the shells all around. Place them evenly. Keep standing back to check the balance.

4 Add the more delicate materials, such as the starfish and thistles, to the top to finish it off.

FRAME WITH GOLDEN SHELLS

Transform a plain, wooden picture frame with gilded seashells, starfish and seaweed. This would be an ideal frame for a mirror. Hang it to allow the gilding to catch the light. As an alternative, use the frame to set off a print or picture with a beach, or maritime theme, or a collage of shoreline treasures.

YOU WILL NEED

MATERIALS
flat-faced wooden frame
acrylic gesso
acrylic paints: titanium white
  and raw sienna
clear matte varnish
3-hour size
Dutch gold leaf transfer book

EQUIPMENT
decorator's and fine
  paintbrushes
paint-mixing container
fine-grade sandpaper
soft pencil
sharp modeling tool

1 Paint the frame with acrylic gesso. Leave to dry. Then make up a creamy wash from diluted white and raw sienna acrylic and paint the frame again. Leave to dry.

2 Lightly sand the frame to distress it slightly and let the wood grain show through. Apply three coats of varnish, allowing each to dry before applying the next.

3 Draw loose, freehand shell, seaweed, and starfish shapes in pencil on the frame.

4 Paint size onto the shapes and, when tacky, gently press gold leaf on to the size. Brush off any excess. Scratch into the gilded surface with the modeling tool for additional texture.

SEASHORE SPONGE-WARE TEA SET

Imagine the effect of a whole tea set of this delightful sponge-ware design, displayed on shelves or a dresser. Painting your own is an inexpensive way of transforming plain, white china, and the end result is a unique one.

YOU WILL NEED

MATERIALS
all-purpose glue
ceramic paints: dark blue and
*   dark green*
white china

EQUIPMENT
ballpoint pen
cellulose kitchen sponge
scissors
corrugated cardboard
paint-mixing container
paper towels
turpentine
rag
fine black felt-tipped pen
stencil brush (optional)
small cosmetic sponge (optional)

1 Draw your crab shape, free-hand, on the sponge. Cut the crab out and glue to a small square of corrugated cardboard. Trim the cardboard as close to the crab as possible. Pour a small amount of blue ceramic paint into the mixing container. Lightly press the sponge into the paint, and blot off any excess paint with paper towels. Gently apply even pressure to stamp the crab onto the china. Carefully lift off the sponge in a single movement.

Repeat the pattern as often as necessary. Remove any mistakes with turpentine on a rag. Set the paint according to the manufacturer's instructions.

2 Draw the border, freehand, around the bottom of the mug with the black pen. Fill in the waves using a stencil brush and set again, according to the instructions.

3 An an alternative, use the cosmetic sponge to sponge the border round the mug. Use both the blue and green paints, to give depth to the border. Set the paint.

SEA-CREATURES WALL DECORATION

This unusual idea for a wall decoration capitalizes on the shininess of ordinary kitchen foil. The effect is shimmering and glittering, with an underwater feel that complements the sea-creatures theme. It can also be done directly on a wall surface.

YOU WILL NEED

MATERIALS
sheet of hardboard
latex paint
gloss paints: dark blue and
 olive green
aluminum foil
clear gloss varnish
artist's oil colors: dark blue
 and chrome yellow

EQUIPMENT
paint-mixing containers
decorator's paintbrush
sponge or rag
thin cardboard or paper
scissors
straight pins
fine paintbrush

1 Paint the hardboard with an undercoat of latex paint. Paint the surface with dark-blue gloss paint. When it is dry, sponge or rag roll the green paint in blotches all over the hardboard.

2 Trace the templates from the back of the book, and enlarge them, if necessary. Cut out the templates very roughly and lay them, face up, on one or two pieces of foil, slightly larger than the templates. Pin the layers together. Cut out the shapes carefully, and separate the layers.

3 Brush some varnish onto the hardboard and apply foil shapes to the surface. Tint some of the varnish with the artist's colors. Add detail and texture with varnish tinted with artist's colors, using a fine paintbrush. When the varnish is dry, give the whole design another coat of tinted varnish.

CUSHION WITH APPLIQUED SEASHELLS

With this lovely cushion cover, the fluid curves of the seashells contrast strikingly with the regularity of the checks.

YOU WILL NEED

MATERIALS
8 in square iron-on fusible bonding web
3 shades of beige cotton scraps
10 in square light-tone cotton gingham
embroidery threads
12 x 16 in medium-tone homespun check
matching thread
24 x 40 in unbleached calico
8 in square dark-tone homespun check

EQUIPMENT
thin cardboard or paper
pencil or fabric marker
scissors
iron and pressing cloth
sewing needle
straight pins
sewing machine
24 buttons

1 Trace the shell templates from the back of the book, and enlarge them, if necessary. Place the bonding web on top of the templates, and trace them onto the fabric with pencil. Cut them out roughly. Iron each shell onto a different scrap of plain cotton fabric. Cut out neatly around each outline.

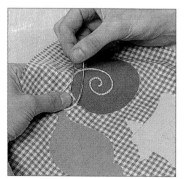

2 Using a fabric marker or sharp pencil, mark the curves and spirals on the right side of the shells. Peel off the backing paper, and arrange the three shapes on the gingham square, using the finished picture as a guide. Fuse by pressing with a cool iron and a pressing cloth.

3 Thread the needle with three strands of embroidery thread and, working with small, regular stitches, embroider a line of chain stitches around the shell shapes to cover the raw edges and pick out the marked details.

▶

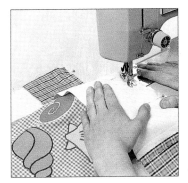

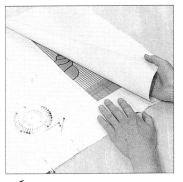

4 Cut two strips of medium-tone cotton, measuring 3 x 10 in. With right sides facing and leaving a seam allowance of ½ in, pin and then sew them to opposite sides of the gingham square. Press the seams open. Cut two further strips, each measuring 3 x 15 in. Pin and then sew them to the remaining two sides of the gingham square. Press the seams open.

5 Cut four 4 x 15 in strips of calico and four 4 in squares of dark-tone cotton. Stitch two strips to opposite sides of the main square, leaving a ½ in seam allowance and press the seams open. Sew a square to each end of the other strips, and press the seams open. With right sides facing, sew in place and press seams open.

6 Cut two rectangles of unbleached calico to make the back of the cushion, each measuring 12 x 18 in. Hem one long side of each. With right sides facing, pin one rectangle to two opposite sides of the cushion front. Sew around the four edges, leaving a ½ in seam allowance. Clip the corners, and turn the cover right side out.

7 Sew the buttons securely along the calico strips at 2 in intervals, using embroidery thread.

SEAHORSE-AND-SEASHELL FRAME

This frame-decorating idea would complement a picture with a seashore subject. It would be equally suitable for a mirror, perhaps in a bathroom with a blue-and-white color scheme. Shells are popular motifs for bathroom fabrics and wallpapers, and this frame would coordinate perfectly.

YOU WILL NEED

MATERIALS
modeling clay
frame
epoxy resin glue
acrylic paints: turquoise, white
  and lemon yellow
gold powder
clear matte varnish

EQUIPMENT
rolling pin
polyethylene sheet (optional)
seashells and seahorse
modeling tools
paint-mixing container
small flat-bristled and fine
  paintbrushes

1 Take a lump of clay and roll it into a ball. Roll the ball into a thick sheet. Press a shell into the clay, to create a negative impression. Repeat with the other shells and the seahorse. Leave to dry for 2–3 days.

2 Take another ball of clay and roll it out in the same way. Press it into the molds, filling the shell and seahorse impressions. Carefully lift off the clay, and place it face up on the work surface.

3 Cut away the excess clay from around each shape. Allow to dry for 2–3 days.

4 Arrange the shapes around the frame, and glue them carefully in position.

▶

5 Mix the acrylic paints to make a turquoise color. To achieve a slight verdigris effect, do not mix the colors too thoroughly. Paint the shapes. Allow to dry.

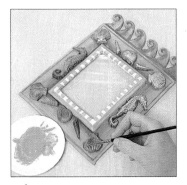

6 Mix the gold powder with varnish, varying the amount of varnish depending on the consistency you want to achieve. Highlight and decorate the shapes with gold.

SEASHELL MIRROR

Decorated with paints and glass "globs," this mirror is cleverly created from molded papier-mâché.

YOU WILL NEED

MATERIALS
strong cardboard
newspaper
wallpaper paste
white glue
white acrylic primer
glass "globs"
epoxy resin glue
gouache paints: deep yellow,
   cadmium yellow, deep cobalt,
   pale blue, Cyprus green,
   grenadine, indigo and white
gold enamel paint
clear gloss and matte varnishes
mirror and fixing-tabs
plate-hanging fixture

FOR THE PAPIER-MACHE PULP
newspaper
2 tablespoons white glue
1 tablespoon linseed oil
few drops oil of cloves
2 tablespoons wallpaper paste

EQUIPMENT
thin cardboard or paper
craft knife
self-healing cutting mat
small and fine paintbrushes
screwdriver

1 Trace the template from the back of the book and enlarge it. Transfer it to the cardboard and cut out. Make the pulp and add to the frame, to build up a 3-D form. Allow to dry.

2 Cover the whole mirror frame with 3–4 layers of newspaper soaked in wallpaper paste. Allow to dry.

3 Coat with white glue and add a coat of primer. When it is dry, attach the glass "globs" with epoxy resin glue. Decorate with gouache paints. Add detail with the gold paint.

4 Paint the frame with several coats of gloss varnish, using matte varnish in places to provide contrast. Allow to dry. Secure the mirror with mirror fixing tabs. Finally, attach the plate-hanging fixture, securing all screws with epoxy resin glue.

PUNCHED-TIN CANDLE HOLDER

Tin punching is a traditional craft typical of the newly fashionable American folk art and it is easy to do. The results are graphic and yet delicately detailed, and the metallic effect will reflect the warm glow of candlelight. Take care not to leave burning candles unattended.

YOU WILL NEED

MATERIALS
aluminum or tin sheet
candle

EQUIPMENT
thin cardboard or paper
marker pen
gloves
tin snips or sharp scissors
magazine or newspaper
large, strong needle
tack hammer
metal ruler
epoxy resin glue
wire brush

1 Trace the template from the back of the book, and enlarge it, if necessary. Transfer the outline to the metal sheet. Wearing gloves, cut it out, using tin snips or sharp scissors.

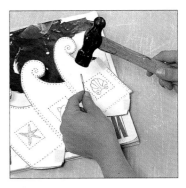

2 Lay the template on a magazine or newspaper to protect the work surface. Using a large, strong needle and a hammer, punch the pattern into the metal sheet.

3 Fold the two outer metal panels inward along the dotted lines, using a metal ruler to crease the sheet cleanly. Do the same with the triangular flaps at the bottom.

4 Overlap the extra lip to secure the triangular shape, and glue it in place. Scratch the surface all over with the wire brush. Put the candle in the bottom of the container.

EMBROIDERED HEM FOR CHILD'S DRESS

Whether a repeat pattern, as illustrated here, or a random one, an embroidered hem is pleasing as a decoration on this denim dress. The shell and starfish shapes are appliquéd and then decorated with embroidery. The embroidered detail helps to unify the whole design and creates a sense of movement throughout.

YOU WILL NEED

MATERIALS
white cotton (ironed)
selection of fabric paints
dress
fabric glue
embroidery threads

EQUIPMENT
lining paper or newspaper
paint-mixing container
paintbrush
iron
tracing paper
pencil
embroidery scissors
selection of needles
towel

1 Lay the cotton on a larger sheet of paper. Paint separate pieces of fabric in different colors. Allow to dry for 24 hours. Then set, according to the paint manufacturer's instructions. Draw starfish and shell shapes on tracing paper.

2 Transfer the shapes several times onto the painted fabric. Cut them out, leaving a ¼ in border outside the outlines. Lay the shapes on the hem of the dress, and design a pleasing pattern. Glue the shapes down sparingly.

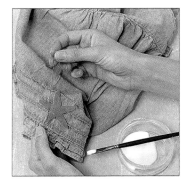

3 Embroider a running stitch or a continuous double running stitch around the template outlines.

4 Embroider details to represent sand, stones, etc. Cut off loose threads, and iron on the wrong side over a towel.

MARITIME TILE MURAL

Four plain ceramic tiles combine to make a striking mural design, reminiscent of Japanese crafts in its graphic simplicity with its clear, calm blue-and-white color scheme. There are many different brands of ceramic paint available. Some are set by baking in the oven while others can just be left to dry.

YOU WILL NEED

MATERIALS
4 white-glazed 6 in square tiles
ceramic paints: medium blue, dark blue and black

EQUIPMENT
soft and hard pencils
tracing paper
masking tape
china marker
paint-mixing container
small and fine paintbrushes

1 Trace the fish template from the back of the book, and enlarge it, if necessary. Tape the tracing to the tiles, positioning it centrally. Transfer the outline to the tiles with a hard pencil.

2 Trace over the outline again with the china marker. Draw the border freehand, and add any extra details to the fish. Follow the finished picture as a guide.

3 Using the ceramic paints, fill in the fish shape. First, paint the main part of the fish medium blue.

4 Paint the detail, and the border with dark blue. Highlight the scales with black. Set the paint following the manufacturer's instructions. The tiles will withstand gentle cleaning.

SEASHELL-STENCILED BEACH BAG

Crisp cream and navy give this smart beach bag a nautical look. Much of the charm of the stenciling lies in combining colors to give a three-dimensional look to the seashell shapes, so it's worth practicing on spare fabric or lining paper first.

YOU WILL NEED

MATERIALS
21½ x 30 in cream cotton drill or denim
2 lengths 6 x 15 in blue cotton drill or denim
dry-fabric stencil paints: dark yellow, dark red and navy blue
white, dark orange and blue sewing threads
2 yd cream cotton cord

EQUIPMENT
scissors
stencil cardboard or acetate sheet
craft knife
self-healing cutting mat
spray mount
3 stencil brushes
iron
sewing machine
straight pins
ruler or tape measure
masking tape

1 Cut the cream fabric in two lengthwise. Trace the stencil from the back of the book, and enlarge it, if necessary. Transfer the outline and cut out from stencil cardboard. Coat the back lightly with spray mount, and stencil five shells on each piece of fabric, using two or three colors. When thoroughly dry, set the paint according to the manufacturer's instructions.

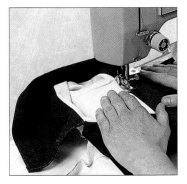

2 Right sides together, sew a blue strip to the top edge of each cream piece, leaving a ½ in seam allowance. Press the seam upward. Pin rectangles right sides together, and stitch around the main bag. Press under the seam allowances on the open sides of the blue fabric, and top stitch in orange. Fold in half lengthwise. Machine stitch parallel to the top stitch.

3 Cut the cord in half, and bind the ends with masking tape. Thread both pieces through the bag. Remove the tape, and bind the ends with blue thread, 2 in from the ends. Fringe and comb the cord to make tassels. Trim neatly.

Sea-creatures Mobile

These charming creatures will be an instant hit with adults and children. In order for the mobile to be well-balanced, the shapes must be hung from the following lengths of thread and from the correct supports: crab, 5½ in; dolphin, 3 in; seaweed, 3 in; seahorse, 4½ in; large fish, 4 in; shell, 5 in; small fish, 3 in; big starfish, 3 in; small starfish, 3 in.

You Will Need

Materials
0.078 in, 0.065 in and 0.047 in thick, galvanized wire
double-sided tape
medium-weight binding wire
aerosol car paints: red, yellow, aquamarine, blue, and green
nylon thread

Equipment
thin cardboard or paper
wire cutters
snub-nosed pliers
half-circle jewelry pliers

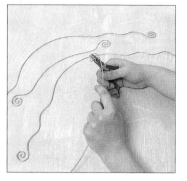

1 To make the small supports, cut two 18 in lengths of 0.078 in wire. Bend each wire into an arch, and form a coil at each end, using snub-nosed pliers. Bend a curve in the wire, beside each coil, using half-round pliers. Make two main supports in the same way from two 29 in lengths of 0.078 in wire. Bend waves in the wire beside each coil.

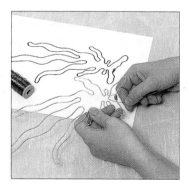

2 Cut a 1¼ in length of 0.078 in wire. Using the half-circle pliers, bend the wire around to make a ring. Cross the main support wires so that they meet exactly in the center, and tape them together with the ring at the top, using double-sided tape. Wrap the binding wire around the joint to secure it, completely covering the double-sided tape.

3 Trace the templates from the back of the book, and enlarge them to 300%. Form each creature by shaping the wire around the template. First, cut a 36 in length of 0.065 in wire. Form it into a seaweed shape, following the template of the book. Join the ends, and wrap them with binding wire.

▶

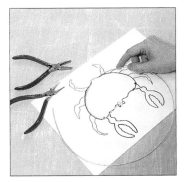

4 Following the template, form the crab's body from a 16 in length of 0.065 in wire. Make an eye loop at each end of the wire.

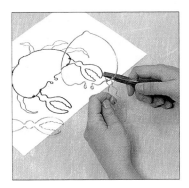

5 Make the front legs from two 11½ in lengths of 0.047 in wire. Twist the ends of the legs around the crab's body, and squeeze to secure.

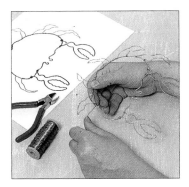

6 Use a continuous length of binding wire to make the back legs. Wrap the wire around the crab's body, between the legs.

7 Follow the templates and use these lengths of 0.065 in wire to make: one shell from 8½ in, two starfish from 13 in and 20 in, and a seahorse from 39 in. Join and wrap the ends

with binding wire. Use binding wire to make the seahorse's fins, nipping a point in each arch with pliers.

Starting at the eyes, make a small fish from 28 in wire and a large fish from 40 in wire. On the large fish, bend the wire to curve across the back. Give each fish a wavy line of binding wire between head and body, binding the joints.

For the dolphin, start at the eye and bend 42½ in wire around the outline to the mouth. Curve the wire back inside the body, finishing at the tail and mouth. Bind the joints.

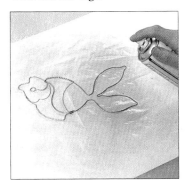

8 Spray paint the creatures in one or two colors. To assemble, follow the finished picture. Attach to the supports, with nylon thread. Use the lengths of thread given on page 51.

SEAHORSE STORAGE BOX

Delicate, swirling brush strokes create a watery background for this delightful seahorse. The box could be used for storing stationery, pencils, jewelry or even cosmetics.

YOU WILL NEED

MATERIALS
¼ in thick pine slat, 27 in long and 1¼ in wide
wood glue
¼ in thick birch-faced plywood sheet, 16 in square
primer
acrylic paints: blue, white, green and gold

EQUIPMENT
ruler
coping saw or fretsaw
medium- and fine-grade sandpaper
masking tape
scissors
pencil
1 in paintbrush
stencil cardboard or acetate sheet
craft knife
self-healing cutting mat
stencil brush

1 Cut two 8 in and two 5½ in lengths of pine with the saw. Sand the rough edges. Glue these together to form the sides of the box. Hold the frame together with masking tape while the glue is drying.

3 Sand the box. Then give it a coat of primer.

2 Place the frame on the plywood, and draw around the inside to mark out the base of the box. Cut out the base. Repeat the process to make the lid insert. Next, draw around the outside of the box and cut out, to make the lid. Glue the base into the frame. Sand around the lid insert, making sure it will fit in the box before gluing it to the lid.

▶

4 When dry, sand the box again, using fine sandpaper. Using two shades of blue acrylic, paint the box with swirling brush strokes.

5 Trace the seahorse template from the back of the book, and enlarge it, if necessary. Transfer the seahorse pattern onto the stencil cardboard or acetate sheet. Carefully cut out the stencil with a sharp, craft knife, using a cutting mat.

6 Tape the stencil onto the lid to hold it firmly in place. Stencil the pattern, using a combination of blue and green acrylic paints. Finish with a very light smattering of gold. When the paint is dry, lightly sand the whole box with fine sandpaper.

SPARKLING STARFISH BROOCH

Layers of contrasting fabrics and glittering machine embroidery make this a spectacular jewelry item. The rough texture of the felts is wonderfully highlighted by the shimmering organdy and metallic-machine embroidery.

YOU WILL NEED

MATERIALS
purple felt
rust felt
shot organdy
metallic embroidery threads
sewing thread
brooch "findings" (backplate and pin)

EQUIPMENT
thin cardboard or paper
scissors
straight pins
dressmaker's chalk
sewing machine with embroidery foot
sewing needle

1 Draw two freehand starfish shapes onto thin cardboard or paper, one larger than the other. Cut the templates out roughly. Pin the large starfish template to the purple felt and draw around it.

2 Cut out irregular pointed shapes from the purple and the rust felt. Pin them down into the points of the starfish outline. Cut out the small starfish shape from the organdy and pin it on top of the felt starfish.

3 Thread the machine with metallic thread, and stitch over the edges of the organdy. Build up layers of texture and color with different threads.

4 Cut out the starfish brooch shape, and stitch a small felt circle onto the center-back. Stitch on the brooch findings.

TEMPLATES

For some of the projects, the templates need to be enlarged to a specific size. For these, the enlargements are given. The rest of the templates can be used at any size.

If the templates need to be enlarged, either use a grid system or a photocopier. For the grid system, trace the template and draw a grid of evenly spaced squares over your tracing. To scale up, draw a larger grid on to another piece of paper. Copy the outline onto the second grid by taking each square individually and drawing the relevant part of the outline in the larger square. Finally, draw over the lines to make sure they are continuous. When tracing the templates, you will need a pencil, tracing paper and scissors.

Maritime Tile Mural, p46

Silk-painted Sheer Curtain, p19

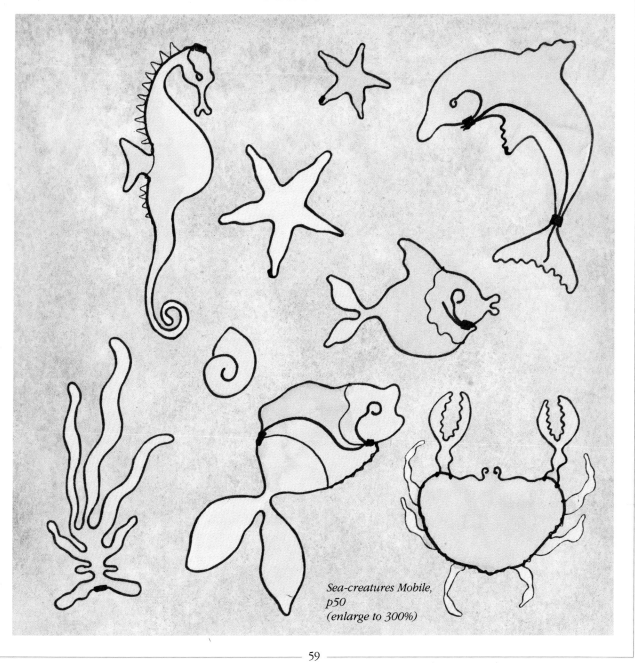

Sea-creatures Mobile,
p50
(enlarge to 300%)

Sea-toned Pillowcase, p24

Seahorse Storage Box,
p53 (enlarge to 160%)

Cushion with Appliquéd Seashells,
p34 (enlarge to 240%)

Pinpricked Lampshade,
p12

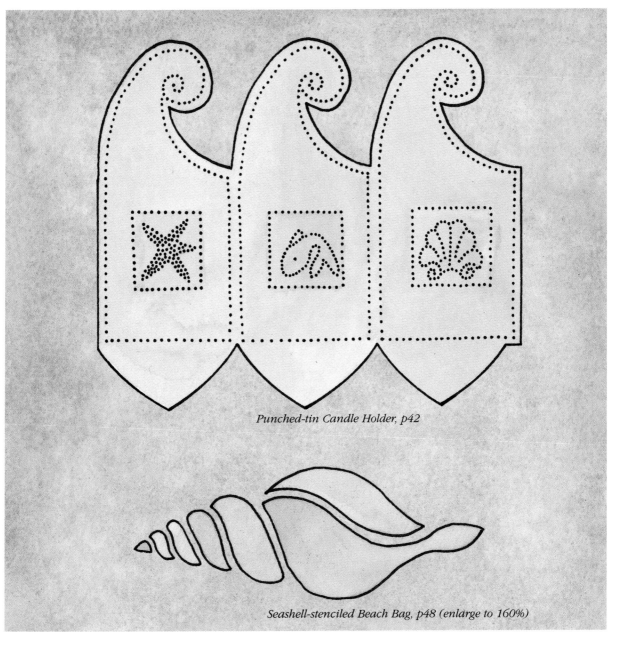

Punched-tin Candle Holder, p42

Seashell-stenciled Beach Bag, p48 (enlarge to 160%)

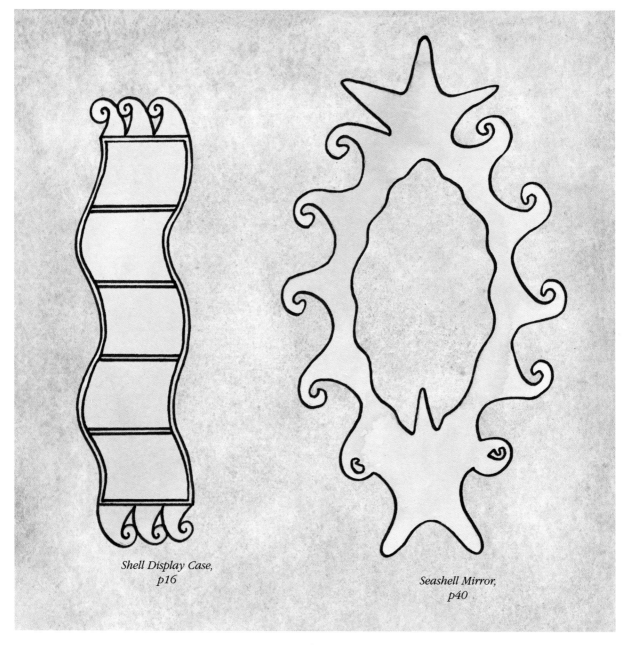

Shell Display Case,
p16

Seashell Mirror,
p40

Sea-creatures Wall Decoration, p32

A

C

B

Hand-printed Seaweed Gift Wrap, p22

ACKNOWLEDGEMENTS

The author and publishers would like to thank the following people for designing the projects in this book:

Ofer Acoo
Shell Display Case pp16–18; Seashore-and-seashell Frame pp37–39

Penny Boylan
Pinpricked Lampshade pp12–13

Louise Brownlow
Silk-painted Sheer Curtain pp19–21; Sea-creatures Wall Decoration pp32–33

Lucinda Ganderton
Cushion with Appliquéd Seashells pp34–36; Seashell-stenciled Beach Bag pp48–49

Louise Gardam
Frame with Golden Shells pp28–29

Dawn Gulyas
Sea-creatures Mobile pp50–52

Jill Hancock
Seahorse Storage Box pp53–55

Abigail Mill
Embroidered Underwater Picture pp14–15; Sparkling Starfish Brooch pp56–57

Terence Moore
Seashell Candle Pot pp26–27

Izzy Moreau
Seashore Sponge-ware Tea Set pp30–31; Maritime Tile Mural pp46–47

Kim Rowley
Seashell Mirror pp40–41

Adele Tipler
Punched-tin Candle Holder pp42–43

Kelie-Marie Townsend
Embroidered Hem for Child's Dress pp44–45

Josephine Whitfield
Hand-printed Seaweed Gift Wrap pp22–23

Dorothy Wood
Sea-toned Pillowcase pp24–25

PICTURE CREDITS
The publishers would like to thank E.T. Archive for the loan of the pictures on pages 8 (top), 10 and 11, the Bridgeman Art Library for the pictures on pages 8 (bottom) and 9 (British Museum), and Archiv Für Kunst Und Geschichte for the picture on page 8 (center).